fondue

A range of simple and delicious

recipes for all kinds of fondues

Lorraine Turner

This is a Parragon Book
First published in 2003

Parragon
Queen Street House
4 Queen Street
Bath BA1 1HE, UK

Copyright © Parragon 2003

Produced by The Bridgewater Book Company Ltd

Main photography by **Calvey Taylor-Haw**
Home economist **Ruth Pollock**

Hardback ISBN: 1-40541-779-X
Paperback ISBN: 1-40541-981-4

Printed in Indonesia

Notes

• This book uses both metric and imperial measurements. Follow the same units of measurement throughout; do not mix metric and imperial.

• All spoon measurements are level: teaspoons are assumed to be 5 ml, and tablespoons are assumed to be 15 ml.

• Unless otherwise stated, milk is assumed to be full fat, eggs and individual vegetables such as potatoes are medium and pepper is freshly ground black pepper.

• Recipes using raw or very lightly cooked eggs should be avoided by infants, the elderly, pregnant women, convalescents and anyone suffering from an illness.

• Optional ingredients, variations or serving suggestions have not been included in the calculations. The times given are an approximate guide only.

contents

introduction

Derived from French — fondue means melted — this creamy mixture of cheese, white wine and flavourings originated in Switzerland. The ingredients are combined in the kitchen, then transferred to a ceramic fondue pot set over a burner. Chunks of bread are speared on long-handled forks and dipped into the pot for a delicious and filling snack. Naturally, traditional fondues are based on Swiss cheeses, such as Gruyère, but modern recipes have introduced all sorts of other types, from fontina to Brie, with their distinctive characteristics. Additional flavourings range from the subtle to the pungent and include garlic, shallots, herbs, kirsch, brandy and cayenne pepper. As this economical rustic dish has become more sophisticated and migrated from the countryside to the city, so the range of dippers has grown, and these days may include pitta bread, garlic bread, olives and raw or lightly cooked vegetables.

Fondues are suitable for a whole host of occasions, from simple, and very social, midweek family suppers to special dinner parties. They also make delicious and unusual dessert courses

Try seafood dippers for a contemporary twist

Ensure meat is cooked through in the oil or stock

Bread is the dipper-of-choice for cheese fondues

Vegetables can be dipped blanched or raw

Fruit dippers are perfect for sweet fondues

The fondue bourguignonne was a later development. Oil is heated in a metal fondue pot, which is then set over a burner. It was originally designed for cooking pieces of steak, before dipping them in sauces and relishes and eating with pickles, mustard and other condiments, but soon all sorts of delicious morsels were being prepared in this way, from fish to tiny spring rolls. Marinating the dippers in advance makes them even tastier and an unusual treat is to coat them in a light batter before frying. A selection of salads and sauces is an easy way to make a fondue party fun.

The third kind of fondue derives from the Mongolian steamboat or firepot and is a popular dish throughout Asia. A variety of ingredients are speared on forks and cooked in a stock in the pot. They may then be combined with other ingredients before being wrapped in Chinese leaves or lettuce parcels, or they may simply be eaten with tasty dipping sauces.

Finally, the dessert fondue was invented. The first choice is invariably chocolate, but toffee and syrup mixtures are also popular. Fresh fruits are easy dippers, but you can also choose biscuits, cakes and fritters.

Enamelled cast iron fondue pots are useful all-rounders, and are the best choice if you plan on cooking a variety of fondues

Stainless steel pots are best for meat fondues. Make sure it has a metal top ring to reduce the risk of being burned by spurts of oil

Earthenware pots are great for cheese and dessert fondues but they cannot stand the temperatures needed for meat fondues

vegetarian fondues

Cheese fondues make delicious, protein-rich meals, and wonderful conversation pieces for social occasions. You can ring the changes by experimenting with different cheeses. For example, many people know about the excellent melting qualities of Gruyère and Emmenthal cheeses, but why not try Italian fontina cheese (see page 14), or a goat's cheese such as Montrachet (see page 24)? For a taste of the east, try Mixed Vegetable Tempura (see page 34) or Mini Spring Rolls (see page 32). And children will love Crispy Edam Melts (see page 30). There's something for everyone here.

GREEK CHEESE WITH OLIVES, PITTA & PEPPERS

INGREDIENTS

1 large garlic clove, finely chopped
225 ml/8 fl oz Greek dry white wine
400 g/14 oz Emmenthal cheese, grated
75 g/2¾ oz feta cheese, crumbled
1½ tbsp cornflour
2 tbsp ouzo
1 tbsp chopped fresh coriander
salt and pepper

Dippers
whole dark kalamata olives, stoned
warmed garlic pitta bread, cut into
    bite-sized pieces
skinned red peppers (see page 24),
    cut into bite-sized pieces

1 Put the garlic and all but 2 tablespoons of the wine into a large saucepan and bring to a gentle simmer over a low heat. Add a small handful of the Emmenthal cheese and stir until melted. Add the remaining Emmenthal gradually, stirring constantly after each addition. Add the feta cheese and stir until melted.

2 In a bowl, mix the cornflour with the ouzo, then stir into the saucepan. Continue to stir for 3–4 minutes, until thickened and bubbling. Stir in the coriander and add salt and pepper to taste.

3 Pour the mixture into a fondue pot and, using protective gloves, transfer to a lit tabletop burner. To serve, allow your guests to spear olives and pieces of pitta bread and red pepper on to fondue forks and dip them into the hot cheese fondue.

WILD MUSHROOM & HERBS WITH VEGETABLES

INGREDIENTS

2 tbsp butter
200 g/7 oz mixed wild mushrooms, such as shiitake, chanterelle and morel, roughly sliced
salt and pepper
1 tbsp chopped fresh parsley
1 tbsp chopped fresh oregano
2 spring onions, trimmed and finely chopped

175 ml/6 fl oz vegetable stock
3 tbsp lemon juice
175 ml/6 fl oz dry white wine
300 g/10½ oz fontina cheese, chopped
300 g/10½ oz Emmenthal cheese, grated
1 tbsp cornflour

Dippers
fresh crusty bread, cut into bite-sized pieces
selection of lightly cooked vegetables, cut into bite-sized pieces

1 Melt the butter in a frying pan over a medium heat. Add the mushrooms and cook, stirring, for 3–4 minutes, until tender. Season to taste with salt and pepper, then stir in the parsley and oregano. Remove from the heat and set aside.

2 Put the spring onions into a flameproof fondue pot and pour in the stock, lemon juice and all but 2 tablespoons of the wine. Transfer to the hob and bring to a gentle simmer over a low heat. Add a small handful of cheese and stir until melted. Repeat until all the cheese has been added and stir until thoroughly melted and bubbling gently. Stir in the reserved mushroom mixture in small batches, until thoroughly incorporated.

3 In a bowl, mix the cornflour with the remaining wine, then stir into the fondue. Continue to stir for 3–4 minutes, until thickened and bubbling. Taste and adjust the seasoning if necessary. Using protective gloves, transfer the fondue pot to a lit tabletop burner. To serve, allow your guests to spear pieces of bread and lightly cooked vegetables on to fondue forks and dip them into the fondue.

GRUYERE & COMTE WITH ASPARAGUS

INGREDIENTS
1 garlic clove, peeled and halved
425 ml/15 fl oz dry white wine
5 tbsp brandy
200 g/7 oz Gruyère cheese, grated
200 g/7 oz Emmenthal cheese,
    grated
200 g/7 oz Comté cheese, grated
100 g/3½ oz Parmesan cheese,
    grated
2 tbsp cornflour
pinch of freshly grated nutmeg
salt and pepper

Dippers
fresh crusty bread, cut into
    bite-sized pieces
small pieces of blanched asparagus

1 Rub the inside of a flameproof fondue pot with the garlic. Discard the garlic. Pour in the wine and 3 tablespoons of the brandy, then transfer to the hob and bring to a gentle simmer over a low heat.

2 Add a small handful of grated cheese and stir constantly until melted. Continue to add the cheese gradually, stirring constantly after each addition. Repeat until all the cheese has been added and stir until thoroughly melted and bubbling gently.

3 In a bowl, mix the cornflour with the remaining brandy. Stir the cornflour mixture into the fondue and continue to stir for 3–4 minutes, until thickened and bubbling. Stir in the nutmeg and season to taste with salt and pepper.

4 Using protective gloves, transfer the fondue pot to a lit tabletop burner. To serve, allow your guests to spear pieces of crusty bread and blanched asparagus on to fondue forks and dip them into the fondue.

BASIL & FONTINA

INGREDIENTS
35 g/1¼ oz fresh basil,
   finely chopped
3 garlic cloves, finely chopped
300 g/10½ oz fontina cheese,
   chopped
250 g/9 oz ricotta cheese
50 g/1¾ oz Parmesan cheese, grated
2 tbsp lemon juice
375 ml/13 fl oz vegetable stock
1 tbsp cornflour
salt and pepper

Dippers
fresh Italian bread, such as
   ciabatta or focaccia, cut
   into bite-sized pieces
selection of lightly cooked
   vegetables, cut into
   bite-sized pieces

1 Put the basil and garlic into a large mixing bowl. Add all the cheeses and stir together well.

2 Put the lemon juice and all but 2 tablespoons of the stock into a large saucepan and bring to a gentle simmer over a low heat. Add a small spoonful of the cheese mixture and stir constantly until melted. Continue to add the cheese mixture gradually, stirring constantly after each addition. Repeat until all the cheese mixture has been added and stir until thoroughly melted and bubbling gently. Mix the cornflour with the remaining stock, then stir into the saucepan. Continue to stir for 3–4 minutes, until thickened and bubbling. Season to taste with salt and pepper.

3 Pour the mixture into a fondue pot and, using protective gloves, transfer to a lit tabletop burner. To serve, allow your guests to spear pieces of bread and vegetables on to fondue forks and dip them into the fondue.

FRENCH CHEESE WITH POTATO & BROCCOLI

INGREDIENTS

2 spring onions, trimmed and chopped
500 ml/18 fl oz dry white wine
350 g/12 oz Beaufort cheese, grated
350 g/12 oz Camembert cheese, rind
   removed, cut into small pieces
2 tbsp cornflour
pinch of cayenne pepper
salt and pepper

Crispy potato skins
750 g/1 lb 10 oz medium potatoes
3 tbsp butter, melted
salt and pepper

Dippers
warm garlic bread or crusty French
   bread, cut into bite-sized pieces
blanched broccoli florets

1 To make the potato skins, preheat the oven to 200°C/400°F/Gas Mark 6. Scrub the potatoes, pierce with a fork and bake in the oven for 50 minutes. Cool, then cut each potato lengthways into 8 pieces. Scoop out most of the cooked potato flesh, but leave a thin layer on each piece. Brush with butter, season with salt and pepper to taste and arrange skin-side down on a baking sheet. Bake at the same temperature for 12–15 minutes, until crisp.

2 Put the spring onions into a flameproof fondue pot with all but 2 tablespoons of the wine. Transfer to the hob and bring to a simmer over a low heat. Add a small handful of cheese and stir until melted. Repeat until all the cheese has been added and is melted and bubbling gently.

3 In a bowl, mix the cornflour with the remaining wine, stir into the fondue and continue to stir for 3–4 minutes, until thickened and bubbling. Stir in the cayenne and salt and pepper to taste. Using protective gloves, transfer the fondue pot to a lit tabletop burner. To serve, allow your guests to spear potato skins, pieces of bread and broccoli florets on to fondue forks and dip them into the fondue.

THREE-CHEESE & BRANDY WITH CARAMELIZED ONIONS

INGREDIENTS

1 garlic clove, finely chopped

425 ml/15 fl oz dry white wine

250 g/9 oz mature Cheddar cheese, grated

250 g/9 oz Wensleydale cheese, crumbled

200 g/7 oz Somerset Brie or other Brie, rind removed, cut into small pieces

1 tbsp cornflour

2 tbsp brandy

salt and pepper

Caramelized onions

1 tbsp butter

1 tbsp olive oil

250 g/9 oz baby onions, peeled but left whole

1 tsp caster sugar

1 tsp balsamic vinegar

Dippers

warm garlic bread, cut into bite-sized pieces

1 First make the caramelized onions. Melt the butter and oil in a frying pan over a medium heat. Add the onions and cook, stirring, for 10 minutes. Sprinkle over the sugar and cook for 5 minutes, then stir in the vinegar. Cook for another 5 minutes, then remove from the heat and set aside.

2 Put the garlic into a flameproof fondue pot and pour in the wine. Transfer to the hob and bring to a gentle simmer over a low heat. Add a small handful of cheese and stir until melted. Continue to add the cheese gradually, stirring constantly after each addition. Repeat until all the cheese has been added and stir until thoroughly melted and the mixture is bubbling gently.

3 In a bowl, mix the cornflour with the brandy. Stir the cornflour mixture into the fondue and continue to stir for 3–4 minutes, until thickened and bubbling. Season to taste. Using protective gloves, transfer the fondue pot to a lit tabletop burner. To serve, allow your guests to spear the caramelized onions and pieces of garlic bread and vegetables on to fondue forks and dip them into the hot fondue.

MUSHROOM WITH POTATO & GARLIC BREAD

INGREDIENTS

3 tbsp butter
100 g/3½ oz button mushrooms, diced
100 g/3½ oz chestnut mushrooms, diced
salt and pepper
1 tbsp chopped fresh parsley

1 garlic clove, finely chopped
450 ml/16 fl oz dry white wine
350 g/12 oz Brie, rind removed, cut into small pieces
350 g/12 oz Beaufort cheese, grated
2 tbsp cornflour
2 tbsp brandy

Dippers
warm garlic bread, cut into bite-sized pieces
baby new potatoes, steamed
small whole mushrooms, lightly sautéed

1 Melt the butter in a frying pan over a medium heat. Add the diced mushrooms and cook, stirring, for 3–4 minutes, until tender. Season to taste with salt and pepper, then stir in the parsley. Remove from the heat and set aside.

2 Put the garlic into a flameproof fondue pot and pour in the wine. Transfer to the hob and bring to a gentle simmer over a low heat. Add a small handful of cheese and stir constantly until melted. Continue to add the cheese gradually, stirring constantly after each addition. Repeat until all the cheese has been added and stir until thoroughly melted and bubbling gently. Stir in the reserved mushroom mixture in small batches, until thoroughly incorporated.

3 In a bowl, mix the cornflour with the brandy. Stir the cornflour mixture into the fondue and continue to stir for 3–4 minutes, until thickened and bubbling. Taste and adjust the seasoning if necessary. Using protective gloves, transfer the fondue pot to a lit tabletop burner. To serve, allow your guests to spear pieces of garlic bread, potatoes and mushrooms on to fondue forks and dip them into the fondue.

PINK CHAMPAGNE & CREAM

INGREDIENTS
400 ml/14 fl oz pink champagne
300 g/10½ oz Gruyère cheese, grated
300 g/10½ oz Crottin de Chavignol cheese, or other goat's cheese if unavailable, cut into small pieces
1 tbsp cornflour
2 tbsp single cream
salt and pepper

Dippers
fresh crusty bread, cut into bite-sized pieces
whole white seedless grapes

1 Pour the champagne into a flameproof fondue pot. Transfer to the hob and bring to a gentle simmer over a low heat. Add a small handful of Gruyère cheese and stir constantly until melted. Continue to add the Gruyère gradually, stirring constantly after each addition. Repeat until all the Gruyère has been added and stir until thoroughly melted and bubbling gently. Stir in the Crottin de Chavignol cheese until melted.

2 In a bowl, mix the cornflour with the cream. Stir the cornflour mixture into the fondue and continue to stir for 3–4 minutes, until thickened and bubbling. Season to taste with salt and pepper.

3 Using protective gloves, transfer the fondue pot to a lit tabletop burner. To serve, allow your guests to spear pieces of bread and grapes on to fondue forks and dip them into the fondue.

RED PEPPER & GARLIC

INGREDIENTS

2 red peppers, cut into quarters
  and deseeded
1 large garlic clove, finely chopped
250 ml/9 fl oz dry white wine
400 g/14 oz Gruyère cheese, grated
75 g/2¾ oz Montrachet cheese, or
  other goat's cheese if unavailable,
  cut into small pieces
1 tbsp cornflour
1 tbsp chopped fresh parsley
salt and pepper

Dippers
whole green and black olives, stoned
fresh crusty bread, cut into
  bite-sized pieces
roasted courgettes, cut into
  bite-sized pieces
red peppers, cut into bite-sized pieces

1 To skin the peppers, flatten them and arrange skin-side up on a grill rack lined with foil. Place under a hot grill for 10–15 minutes, until the skins are blackened. Transfer to a polythene bag, set aside for 15 minutes, then peel off the skins. Cut six of the pieces into bite-sized chunks and reserve for dippers. Finely dice the remaining pepper pieces.

2 Put the garlic and all but 2 tablespoons of the wine into a large saucepan and bring to a gentle simmer over a low heat. Add a small handful of the Gruyère cheese and stir until melted. Add the remaining Gruyère gradually, stirring constantly after each addition. Add the diced red pepper, then stir in the Montrachet until melted.

3 In a bowl, mix the cornflour with the remaining wine, add to the saucepan and stir for 3–4 minutes, until thickened and bubbling. Stir in the parsley and add salt and pepper to taste. Pour the mixture into a fondue pot and, using protective gloves, transfer to a lit tabletop burner. To serve, allow your guests to spear olives and pieces of bread, red pepper and courgette on to fondue forks and dip them into the fondue.

RAVIOLI WITH RED WINE STOCK

INGREDIENTS

Stock
1 garlic clove, chopped
2 onions, chopped
2 celery sticks, chopped
3 large carrots, peeled and chopped
1.2 litres/2 pints water
1 bay leaf
3 fresh parsley sprigs
salt and pepper
3 tbsp red wine

Ravioli
450 g/1 lb durum wheat flour
4 eggs, beaten
2 tbsp olive oil
1 onion, finely chopped
4 tomatoes, peeled and
    finely chopped
100 g/3½ oz mushrooms,
    finely chopped
200 g/7 oz spinach leaves, blanched
    and finely chopped
50 g/1¾ oz Parmesan cheese, grated
2 tbsp chopped fresh basil

Dippers
selection of blanched vegetables,
    cut into bite-sized pieces

1 To make the ravioli, sift the flour into a mound on a clean work surface and make a well in the centre. Add the eggs and half the oil. Mix together well. Knead for 10 minutes, then set aside for 30 minutes. Halve the dough, then roll out thinly into 2 rectangles. Cover with a damp tea towel.

2 In a frying pan, cook the onion, tomatoes and mushrooms in the remaining oil over a medium heat for 8–10 minutes, or until the liquid has evaporated. Mix with the remaining ravioli ingredients, then place spoonfuls at regular intervals on one pasta rectangle. Cover with the other rectangle, cut into squares around the mounds and seal. Set aside.

3 To make the stock, bring all the ingredients to the boil in a saucepan, then reduce the heat and simmer for 1 hour. Strain through a sieve into a heatproof bowl. Discard the solids. Pour the liquid into a flameproof fondue pot until two-thirds full, then bring to boiling point on the hob. Using protective gloves, transfer the fondue pot to a lit tabletop burner. To serve, allow your guests to spear the ravioli and vegetables on to fondue forks and dip in the hot stock until cooked to their taste.

SPRING ONION & LEEK WITH TOFU

INGREDIENTS

6 spring onions, trimmed and chopped
1 leek, trimmed and sliced
2 celery sticks
3 large carrots, peeled and chopped
1.2 litres/2 pints water
1 bouquet garni, made from fresh
   parsley, thyme and rosemary sprigs
   and a bay leaf
salt and pepper
1 garlic clove, peeled and halved
1 tbsp sherry

Dippers

200 g/7 oz firm tofu (drained
   weight), cut into bite-sized pieces
selection of vegetables, such as
   broccoli florets and button
   mushrooms, and red peppers,
   cut into bite-sized pieces

1 Put the spring onions, leek, celery sticks, carrots and water into a large saucepan. Add the bouquet garni, season to taste with salt and pepper and bring to the boil, then reduce the heat and simmer for 1 hour. Remove from the heat and strain through a sieve into a large heatproof bowl. Discard the solids and reserve the liquid. Arrange the dippers on a large serving platter or individual plates ready for cooking.

2 Rub the inside of a flameproof fondue pot with the garlic. Discard the garlic. Pour in the reserved liquid until the fondue pot is two-thirds full, then transfer to the hob and bring to boiling point over a medium heat. Stir in the sherry. Using protective gloves, transfer the fondue pot to a lit tabletop burner. To serve, allow your guests to spear the dippers on to fondue forks and dip them in the hot stock until cooked to their taste.

CRISPY EDAM MELTS

INGREDIENTS

250 g/9 oz plain flour

¼ tsp cayenne pepper

400 g/14 oz Edam cheese, rind removed
   and cut into bite-sized cubes

1 tsp baking powder

1 tsp salt

2 large eggs

125 ml/4 fl oz milk

1 litre/1¾ pints groundnut oil

Dippers

whole button mushrooms

whole cherry tomatoes

blanched broccoli florets

fresh mixed salad, to serve

1 Sift 150 g/5½ oz of the flour with the cayenne pepper into a large bowl. Add the cheese cubes and turn until coated. Shake off the excess flour, then arrange the cheese on a serving platter.

2 Put the remaining flour into a large bowl with the baking powder and salt, then gradually beat in the eggs, milk and 1 tablespoon of the oil. Beat until the batter is smooth, then pour the batter into a serving bowl.

3 Pour the remaining oil into a metal fondue pot (it should be no more than one-third full), then heat on the hob to 190°C/375°F, or until a cube of bread browns in 30 seconds. Using protective gloves, carefully transfer the fondue pot to a lit tabletop burner. To serve, allow your guests to spear the cheese cubes on to fondue forks, dip in the batter and let the excess run off, then cook in the hot oil for 1 minute, or until golden and crisp. Cook the other dippers in the same way, or leave them without batter and cook to your taste. Drain off the excess oil and serve with a fresh mixed salad.

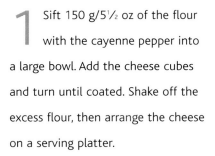

MINI SPRING ROLLS

INGREDIENTS

2 tbsp chilli oil
4 spring onions, trimmed and
   finely chopped
1 red pepper, deseeded and finely sliced
   into 5-cm/2-inch lengths
1 carrot, peeled and finely sliced into
   5-cm/2-inch lengths
85 g/3 oz beansprouts

1 tbsp lemon juice
1 tsp soy sauce
salt and pepper
8 sheets filo pastry, halved
2 tbsp butter, melted
1 egg white, slightly beaten
1 litre/1¾ pints groundnut oil

Dippers
selection of vegetables, cut into
   bite-sized pieces

To serve
1 quantity Oriental Dipping Sauce
   (see page 38)
freshly cooked rice

1 Heat the chilli oil in a wok or large frying pan. Add the spring onions, red pepper and carrot and stir-fry for 2 minutes. Add the beansprouts, lemon juice and soy sauce and stir-fry for 1 minute, then season to taste with salt and pepper and remove from the heat.

2 Spread out the pastry on a clean work surface and brush with melted butter. Spoon a little of the vegetable mixture on to one short end of each sheet of pastry, fold in the long sides and roll up to enclose the filling. Brush the edges with egg white to seal.

3 Pour the groundnut oil into a metal fondue pot (it should be no more than one-third full), then heat on the hob to 190°C/375°F, or until a cube of bread browns in 30 seconds. Using protective gloves, transfer the fondue pot to a lit tabletop burner. To serve, allow your guests to spear the spring rolls and dippers on to fondue forks and dip into the hot oil until cooked to their taste (the spring rolls will need 2–3 minutes). Drain off the excess oil and serve with the dipping sauce and rice.

MIXED VEGETABLE TEMPURA

INGREDIENTS
6 tbsp cornflour
6 tbsp soy sauce
6 tbsp lemon juice
1 litre/1¾ pints groundnut oil
1 egg
225 ml/8 fl oz ice-cold water
140 g/5 oz plain flour

Dippers
broccoli florets
button mushrooms
aubergine, cut into bite-sized pieces
baby corn cobs, halved
mangetout
cherry tomatoes

freshly cooked noodles, to serve

1 Put the cornflour into a bowl and turn all the vegetable dippers in it until coated. Shake off the excess cornflour, then arrange them on a serving platter. In a serving bowl, make a dipping sauce by mixing together the soy sauce and lemon juice, then set aside.

2 Pour the oil into a metal fondue pot (it should be no more than one-third full), then heat on the hob to 190°C/375°F, or until a cube of bread browns in 30 seconds. Using protective gloves, carefully transfer the fondue pot to a lit tabletop burner.

3 In a separate serving bowl, beat the egg and water together, then stir in the flour briefly. Do not overbeat: the batter should be lumpy. To serve, allow your guests to spear the dippers on to fondue forks, dip them in the batter and let the excess run off, then cook in the hot oil for 2–3 minutes, or until cooked to their taste. Drain off the excess oil, then serve the tempura with the dipping sauce and noodles.

AÏOLI

INGREDIENTS
3 large garlic cloves, finely chopped
2 egg yolks
225 ml/8 fl oz extra virgin olive oil
1 tbsp lemon juice
1 tbsp lime juice
1 tbsp Dijon mustard
1 tbsp chopped fresh tarragon
salt and pepper
sprig of tarragon, to decorate

1 Ensure the ingredients are at room temperature. Put the chopped garlic and the egg yolks into a food processor and process until well blended. With the motor running, pour in the olive oil teaspoon-by-teaspoon through the feeder tube until the liquid starts to thicken, then pour in the remaining oil in a thin stream until a thick mayonnaise forms.

2 Add the lemon and lime juices, along with the mustard and tarragon, and season to taste with salt and pepper. Blend until smooth, then transfer to a non-metallic bowl. Decorate with a sprig of tarragon.

3 Cover with clingfilm and refrigerate until needed.

ORIENTAL DIPPING SAUCE

INGREDIENTS

100 ml/3½ fl oz rice wine vinegar
finely grated rind and juice of 1 lime
2 tbsp soy sauce
250 g/9 oz granulated sugar
1 tbsp grated fresh root ginger
1 tbsp grated fresh lemon grass
2 garlic cloves, crushed
1 fresh red chilli, deseeded and
   finely chopped
2 tbsp sherry
1 tbsp chopped fresh coriander

1 Put the vinegar, lime rind and juice, soy sauce and sugar into a small saucepan and place over a medium heat. Stir in the ginger, lemon grass, garlic and chilli and bring to the boil, stirring constantly. Reduce the heat and simmer, stirring, for 5 minutes.

2 Stir in the sherry and coriander, heat through for another minute, then remove from the heat and strain into a heatproof non-metallic serving bowl.

3 Leave to cool to room temperature, then serve.

meat fondues

Beef, pork and chicken are favourite meats for fondues. For a special occasion the Sizzling Steak with Rich Tomato Sauce (see page 56) is unbeatable, or try the ever-popular Chilli & Coriander Pork Satay (see page 60). Oil fondues offer an exciting and dramatic way to present food to your guests. Remember to use a sturdy metal fondue pot and place it securely, with its burner, on a heatproof surface where it cannot be knocked over. Pat dry with kitchen paper any marinated foods before immersing them in the hot oil, otherwise they may splutter and splash your guests.

BLUE CHEESE WITH HAM-WRAPPED DIPPERS

INGREDIENTS
1 garlic clove, peeled and halved
425 ml/15 fl oz dry white wine
5 tbsp brandy
350 g/12 oz Gruyère cheese, grated
350 g/12 oz dolcelatte cheese,
    crumbled
1 tbsp cornflour
2 tbsp single cream
salt and pepper

Dippers
fresh crusty bread, cut into
    bite-sized pieces
bite-sized pieces of lightly cooked
    vegetables wrapped in cooked ham
    or strips of lightly cooked bacon

1 Rub the inside of a flameproof fondue pot with the garlic. Discard the garlic. Pour in the wine and 3 tablespoons of the brandy, then transfer to the hob and bring to a gentle simmer over a low heat. Add a small handful of cheese and stir constantly until melted. Continue to add the cheese gradually, stirring constantly after each addition, until all the cheese has been added. Stir until thoroughly melted and bubbling gently.

2 In a bowl, mix the cornflour with the remaining brandy. Stir the cornflour mixture into the fondue and continue to stir for 3–4 minutes, until thickened and bubbling. Stir in the cream and season to taste with salt and pepper.

3 Using protective gloves, transfer the fondue pot to a lit tabletop burner. To serve, allow your guests to spear pieces of bread and ham-wrapped vegetables on to fondue forks and dip them into the fondue.

SMOKED CHEDDAR WITH HAM & APPLE

INGREDIENTS
2 tbsp lime juice
475 ml/17 fl oz dry cider
700 g/1 lb 9 oz smoked Cheddar
  cheese, grated
2 tbsp cornflour
pinch of ground mixed spice
salt and pepper

Dippers
4 apples, cored and cut into
  bite-sized cubes, then brushed
  with lemon juice
fresh crusty bread, cut into
  bite-sized cubes
canned pineapple chunks, drained
lean cooked ham, cut into
  bite-sized cubes

1 Put the lime juice and all but 2 tablespoons of the cider into a large saucepan and bring to a gentle simmer over a low heat. Add a small handful of the cheese and stir until melted. Add the remaining cheese gradually, stirring constantly after each addition.

2 In a bowl, mix the cornflour with the remaining cider, then stir into the saucepan. Continue to stir for 3–4 minutes, until thickened and bubbling. Stir in the mixed spice and add salt and pepper to taste.

3 Pour the mixture into a fondue pot and, using protective gloves, transfer to a lit tabletop burner. To serve, allow your guests to spear pieces of apple, bread, pineapple and ham on to fondue forks and dip them into the hot fondue.

ITALIAN CHEESE WITH MEAT DIPPERS

INGREDIENTS

1 garlic clove, peeled and halved

450 ml/16 fl oz milk

3 tbsp brandy

300 g/10½ oz dolcelatte cheese,
  crumbled

200 g/7 oz fontina cheese, chopped

200 g/7 oz mozzarella cheese, chopped

1 tbsp cornflour

salt and pepper

Dippers

fresh Italian bread, cut into
  bite-sized pieces

salami, cut into bite-sized pieces

small pieces of apple, wrapped in
  Parma ham

morsels of roast chicken

1 Rub the inside of a flameproof fondue pot with the garlic. Discard the garlic. Pour in the milk and 1 tablespoon of the brandy, then transfer to the hob and bring to a gentle simmer over a low heat.

2 Add a small handful of cheese and stir constantly until melted. Continue to add the cheese gradually, stirring constantly after each addition. Repeat until all the cheese has been added and stir until thoroughly melted and the mixture is bubbling gently.

3 In a bowl, mix the cornflour with the remaining brandy. Stir the cornflour mixture into the fondue and continue to stir for 3–4 minutes, until thickened and bubbling. Season to taste with salt and pepper.

4 Using protective gloves, transfer the fondue pot to a lit tabletop burner. To serve, allow your guests to spear pieces of bread, salami, ham-wrapped apple, and chicken on to fondue forks and dip them into the fondue.

SPANISH MANCHEGO WITH CHORIZO & OLIVES

INGREDIENTS

1 garlic clove, peeled and halved
425 ml/15 fl oz Spanish dry white wine
finely grated rind of 1 lemon or lime
700 g/1 lb 9 oz manchego cheese,
    grated
2 tbsp cornflour
salt and pepper

Dippers

fresh crusty bread, cut into
    bite-sized pieces
chorizo sausage, cut into
    bite-sized pieces and lightly
    fried in olive oil
whole green and black olives, stoned

1 Rub the inside of a flameproof fondue pot with the garlic. Discard the garlic. Pour in the white wine and add the lemon rind, then transfer the fondue pot to the hob and bring to a gentle simmer over a low heat.

2 Toss the cheese in the cornflour, then gradually stir the cheese into the heated liquid, stirring constantly, until the cheese has melted and the liquid is bubbling gently. Stir until thick and creamy. Season to taste with salt and pepper.

3 Using protective gloves, transfer the fondue pot to a lit tabletop burner. To serve, allow your guests to spear pieces of bread and chorizo and whole olives on to fondue forks and dip them into the fondue.

SHABU SHABU

INGREDIENTS

1 litre/1¾ pints beef stock
13-cm/5-inch piece kombu (dried kelp),
    cut into small pieces and rinsed in
    cold water
5 tbsp soy sauce
6 tbsp lime juice
400 g/14 oz precooked udon noodles

Dippers
800 g/1 lb 12 oz beef sirloin, cut into
    thin, bite-sized strips
200 g/7 oz firm tofu (drained
    weight), cut into bite-sized pieces
8 spring onions, trimmed and cut
    into bite-sized pieces

1 Pour the stock into a large saucepan and add the kombu. Bring to the boil, then reduce the heat and simmer for 5 minutes. Meanwhile, mix the soy sauce and lime juice in a small heatproof bowl, then stir in 1 tablespoon of stock from the saucepan and set aside. Arrange the beef, tofu and onion dippers on serving plates.

2 Pour the stock and kombu into a flameproof fondue pot (it should be no more than two-thirds full). Using protective gloves, transfer the fondue pot to a lit tabletop burner. To serve, allow your guests to spear the dippers on to fondue forks or place them on heatproof spoons, dip them into the hot stock until cooked to their taste (cook the beef right through), then dip them in the soy sauce mixture. When all the dippers have been finished, add the noodles to the stock in the fondue pot and serve as a soup.

CHILLI PORK WITH PEANUT SAUCE

INGREDIENTS

4 tbsp lime juice
3 tbsp chilli oil
1 garlic clove, chopped
3 tbsp chopped fresh coriander
600 g/1 lb 5 oz pork fillet, cut into
    thin slices
4 spring onions, trimmed and sliced
1.2 litres/2 pints chicken stock or
    vegetable stock
1 tbsp grated fresh lemon grass
½ tsp chilli powder
salt and pepper

Peanut sauce
250 ml/9 fl oz coconut milk
1 tsp red curry paste
4 tbsp smooth peanut butter
1 tsp grated fresh root ginger

Dippers
200 g/7 oz firm tofu (drained
    weight), cut into bite-sized pieces
selection of blanched vegetables,
    cut into bite-sized pieces

freshly cooked noodles, to serve

1 Pour the lime juice into a large, shallow non-metallic dish. Add half of the oil, the garlic, coriander and pork. Turn the pork in the mixture, cover with clingfilm and refrigerate for 1¼ hours.

2 Heat the remaining oil in a large saucepan over a medium heat. Add the spring onions and cook, stirring, for 3 minutes. Add the stock, lemon grass, chilli powder and salt and pepper to taste. Bring to the boil, then reduce the heat and simmer for 25 minutes. Meanwhile, to make the sauce, simmer the coconut milk in a separate saucepan for 15 minutes, then gradually stir in the curry paste, peanut butter and fresh root ginger and simmer for 5 minutes. Drain the pork and thread on to wooden skewers.

3 Pour the stock mixture into a flameproof fondue pot (it should be no more than two-thirds full). Using protective gloves, transfer to a lit tabletop burner. To serve, allow your guests to spear the dippers on to fondue forks and dip them into the hot stock with the pork skewers until cooked to their taste (cook the pork right through). Serve with noodles and the sauce.

MARINATED BEEF WITH ORIENTAL DIPPING SAUCE

INGREDIENTS

6 tbsp soy sauce
5 tbsp dry sherry
1 garlic clove, chopped
1 tbsp grated fresh root ginger
1 tsp sugar
800 g/1 lb 12 oz fillet steak,
    cut into thin, bite-sized strips
1 litre/1¾ pints groundnut oil

Dippers
selection of vegetables, cut into
    bite-sized pieces

To serve
1 quantity Oriental Dipping Sauce
    (see page 38)
freshly cooked noodles

1 Put the soy sauce, sherry, garlic, ginger and sugar into a large shallow dish and mix together. Add the strips of steak and turn them in the mixture. Cover with clingfilm and refrigerate for 1¼ hours.

2 Drain the steak, pat dry with kitchen paper and thread on to wooden skewers, leaving plenty of space at either end. Arrange the skewers on serving plates with the other dippers. Pour the oil into a metal fondue pot (it should be no more than one-third full), then heat on the hob to 190°C/375°F, or until a cube of bread browns in 30 seconds. Using protective gloves, carefully transfer the fondue pot to a lit tabletop burner.

3 To serve, allow your guests to spear the dippers on to fondue forks and dip them into the hot oil with the beef skewers until cooked to their taste (cook the beef right through). Drain off the excess oil, then serve with the dipping sauce and noodles.

SIZZLING STEAK WITH RICH TOMATO SAUCE

INGREDIENTS

800 g/1 lb 12 oz fillet steak,
    cut into 2-cm/¾-inch cubes
1 litre/1¾ pints groundnut oil
salt and pepper

Rich tomato sauce
1 tbsp olive oil
1 garlic clove, finely chopped
1 onion, finely chopped
400 g/14 oz canned
    chopped tomatoes
1 tbsp tomato purée
2 tbsp red wine
1 tbsp chopped fresh parsley
1 tbsp chopped fresh oregano

Dippers
baby onions, peeled but left whole
button mushrooms
cherry tomatoes

crusty French bread, to serve

1 First make the tomato sauce. Heat the olive oil in a small saucepan over a medium heat, add the garlic and onion and cook, stirring, for 3 minutes, until softened. Stir in the tomatoes, tomato purée and wine. Bring to the boil, then reduce the heat and simmer gently, stirring occasionally, for about 25 minutes. Remove from the heat, stir in the parsley and oregano and set aside. Arrange the cubes of steak and the other dippers on serving plates.

2 Pour the groundnut oil into a metal fondue pot (it should be no more than one-third full), then heat on the hob to 190°C/375°F, or until a cube of bread browns in 30 seconds. Using protective gloves, carefully transfer the fondue pot to a lit tabletop burner.

3 To serve, allow your guests to spear the steak cubes and dippers on to fondue forks and dip them into the hot oil until cooked to their taste (cook the steak right through). Drain off the excess oil, season to taste with salt and pepper, then serve with bread and the tomato sauce (you can serve the sauce hot or cold).

CRISPY-COATED PORK SAUSAGES

INGREDIENTS
450 g/1 lb pork sausagemeat
1 small onion, grated
6 tbsp grated Cheddar cheese
1 tbsp tomato purée
25 g/1 oz fresh breadcrumbs
1 tsp turmeric
½ tsp paprika
salt and pepper
2 eggs, beaten
100 g/3½ oz dried breadcrumbs
1 litre/1¾ pints groundnut oil

Dippers
button mushrooms
aubergine, cut into bite-sized pieces

To serve
1 quantity Mustard Dip (see page 68)
1 quantity Crispy Potato Skins
  (see page 16)
warm crusty bread

1 Put the sausagemeat into a large bowl with the onion, cheese, tomato purée, fresh breadcrumbs, turmeric and paprika, and season to taste with salt and pepper. Mix together well and, using your hands, shape into small sausages about 5 cm/2 inches long. Turn them in the beaten egg, then coat them in dried breadcrumbs. Arrange the sausages on a serving platter with the other dippers.

2 Pour the oil into a metal fondue pot (it should be no more than one-third full), then heat on the hob to 190°C/375°F, or until a cube of bread browns in 30 seconds. Using protective gloves, carefully transfer the fondue pot to a lit tabletop burner.

3 To serve, allow your guests to spear the pork sausages and other dippers on to fondue forks and dip into the hot oil until cooked to their taste (cook the sausages right through – they will need at least 3–4 minutes). Drain off the excess oil, then serve with the dip, bread and Crispy Potato Skins.

CHILLI & CORIANDER PORK SATAY

INGREDIENTS

2 tbsp lemon juice

3 tbsp vegetable oil

1 garlic clove, chopped

2 tbsp chopped fresh coriander

1 tbsp grated fresh lemon grass

1 fresh red chilli, deseeded and
finely chopped

800 g/1 lb 12 oz pork fillet, cut into
thin slices

1 litre/1¾ pints groundnut oil

salt and pepper

Satay sauce

1 tsp chilli oil

1 garlic clove, crushed

1 spring onion, trimmed and
finely chopped

1 fresh red chilli, deseeded and
finely chopped

1 tsp Thai red curry paste

5 tbsp crunchy peanut butter

250 ml/9 fl oz coconut milk

Dippers

selection of fresh vegetables,
cut into bite-sized pieces

freshly cooked rice, to serve

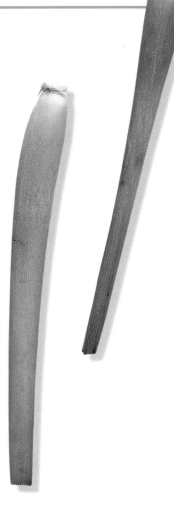

1 Pour the lemon juice into a large, shallow non-metallic dish. Add the vegetable oil, garlic, coriander, lemon grass, chilli and pork. Turn the pork in the mixture, cover with clingfilm and refrigerate for 1¼ hours. Drain the pork, pat dry with kitchen paper and arrange on a serving platter with the other dippers.

2 To make the sauce, heat the chilli oil in a small saucepan, add the garlic and spring onion and cook, stirring, for 3 minutes. Stir in the remaining sauce ingredients, bring to the boil, then reduce the heat to a simmer.

3 Pour the groundnut oil into a metal fondue pot (it should be no more than one-third full), then heat on the hob to 190°C/375°F, or until a cube of bread browns in 30 seconds. Using protective gloves, carefully transfer the fondue pot to a lit tabletop burner. To serve, allow your guests to spear the pork and dippers on to fondue forks and dip into the hot oil until cooked to their taste (cook the pork right through). Drain off the excess oil, season to taste with salt and pepper, then serve with rice and the hot sauce.

SHERRIED ROAST CHICKEN

INGREDIENTS
1 litre/1¾ pints chicken stock
100 ml/3½ fl oz white wine
1 large garlic clove, chopped
1 tsp sugar
4 tbsp sherry

Dippers
750 g/1 lb 10 oz roast chicken breast,
    cut into bite-sized pieces
2 red peppers, skinned (see page 24)
    and cut into bite-sized pieces
blanched broccoli and
    cauliflower florets
peeled carrots, blanched and cut into
    bite-sized pieces

1 quantity Aïoli (see page 36),
    to serve

1 Pour the stock into a large saucepan and add the wine, garlic and sugar. Bring to the boil, then reduce the heat and simmer for 10 minutes. Arrange the dippers on serving plates.

2 Stir the sherry into the stock, then pour the stock into a flameproof fondue pot (it should be no more than two-thirds full). Using protective gloves, transfer the fondue pot to a lit tabletop burner. To serve, allow your guests to spear the dippers on to fondue forks, dip them into the hot stock until cooked to their taste, then dip them in the Aïoli.

SPICY CHICKEN WITH PEPPERS

INGREDIENTS

4 tbsp chilli oil

1 tbsp lemon juice

2 garlic cloves, chopped

½ tsp paprika

½ tsp turmeric

6 skinless, boneless chicken breasts, halved

salt and pepper

850 ml/1½ pints chicken stock

100 ml/3½ fl oz red wine

1 fresh red chilli, deseeded and finely chopped

1 tbsp tomato purée

few drops of red food colouring (optional)

1 tbsp cornflour

Dippers

whole cherry tomatoes

whole black olives, stoned

1 red pepper, skinned (see page 24) and cut into bite-sized pieces

1 orange pepper, skinned (see page 24) and cut into bite-sized pieces

freshly cooked rice, to serve

1 Place the oil, lemon juice and half of the garlic in a large, shallow non-metallic dish. Rub the chicken with the paprika and turmeric, then add to the oil mixture with salt and pepper to taste. Turn until coated. Cover with clingfilm and refrigerate for 1¼ hours.

2 Pour the stock into a large saucepan and pour in all but 2 tablespoons of the wine. Add the chilli, tomato purée, remaining garlic and the food colouring, if using. Bring to the boil, then reduce the heat and simmer for 10 minutes. Drain the chicken, cut into thin, bite-sized slices and arrange on serving plates with the dippers.

3 In a bowl, mix the cornflour with the remaining wine, then stir into the saucepan. Continue to stir for 3–4 minutes, until thickened, then pour into a flameproof fondue pot (it should be no more than two-thirds full). Using protective gloves, transfer the fondue pot to a lit tabletop burner. To serve, allow your guests to spear the dippers on to fondue forks and dip them into the hot stock until cooked to their taste (cook the chicken right through). Serve with rice.

CHILLI CHICKEN FIREPOT

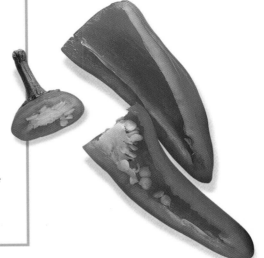

INGREDIENTS

250 g/9 oz rice noodles

4 tbsp lemon juice

3 tbsp vegetable oil

1 fresh red chilli, deseeded and
    finely chopped

1 garlic clove, chopped

3 tbsp chopped fresh coriander

6 skinless, boneless chicken breasts,
    cut into thin, bite-sized slices

4 spring onions, trimmed and sliced

1.2 litres/2 pints chicken stock or
    vegetable stock

1 tbsp grated fresh lemon grass

½ tsp chilli powder

salt and pepper

Dippers

selection of blanched vegetables,
    cut into bite-sized pieces

whole cooked peeled prawns

1 quantity Oriental Dipping Sauce
    (see page 38), to serve

1 Place the noodles in a heatproof bowl, cover with boiling water and soak for 4 minutes. Drain and set aside. Pour the lemon juice into a large, shallow non-metallic dish. Pour in half of the oil, then add the chilli, garlic, coriander and chicken. Turn the chicken in the mixture, cover with clingfilm and refrigerate for 1¼ hours.

2 Heat the remaining oil in a large saucepan over a medium heat. Add the spring onions and cook, stirring, for 3 minutes. Add the stock, lemon grass, chilli powder and salt and pepper to taste. Bring to the boil, then reduce the heat and simmer for 25 minutes. Drain the chicken and arrange on serving plates with the dippers.

3 Pour the stock into a flameproof fondue pot (it should be no more than two-thirds full), then using protective gloves, transfer to a lit tabletop burner. To serve, allow your guests to spear the dippers on to fondue forks, dip them into the hot stock until cooked to their taste (cook the chicken right through), then dip in the dipping sauce. When the dippers are finished, add the noodles to the stock and serve as a soup.

CHICKEN & BACON SKEWERS

INGREDIENTS

½ tsp turmeric
6 skinless, boneless chicken breasts
salt and pepper
1 litre/1¾ pints groundnut oil

Mustard dip
4 tbsp soured cream
4 tbsp mayonnaise
2 tbsp wholegrain mustard
1 tsp honey
1 spring onion, trimmed and
  finely chopped
pinch of paprika

Dippers
4 rashers unsmoked streaky bacon
cherry tomatoes
whole baby onions, peeled
button mushrooms

sautéed new potatoes and a fresh
  mixed salad, to serve

1 Rub the turmeric over the chicken breasts, then season to taste with salt and pepper and cut into strips. Stretch the bacon rashers until doubled in length and cut into thin strips lengthways. Roll up the slices of chicken and bacon, and thread them on to wooden skewers with some of the other dippers, leaving plenty of space at either end (skewer the tomatoes separately as they will need less time to cook). Mix all the ingredients for the dip together in a serving bowl.

2 Pour the oil into a metal fondue pot (it should be no more than one-third full), then heat on the hob to 190°C/375°F, or until a cube of bread browns in 30 seconds. Using protective gloves, carefully transfer the fondue pot to a lit tabletop burner.

3 Allow guests to dip the skewers into the hot oil and cook for 2–3 minutes, or until cooked to individual taste. It is important that the chicken and bacon is cooked right through. Drain off the excess oil, then serve with sautéed potatoes, a mixed salad and the dip.

seafood fondues

Fondues are a great way of serving fish and shellfish as the food is cooked quickly and so stays succulent and full of flavour. Stock fondues are also known as 'Chinese firepots', and are a wonderfully healthy way to cook food – infusing each morsel with exciting flavours. The Oriental Firepot with Seafood Dippers (see page 76) is a great example. For a dish full of zing, nothing beats Pecorino & Chilli Tuna Sizzlers (see page 78) served with a red chilli dipping sauce. Light and fresh, seafood fondues ensure that any party gets off to a sizzling start.

KOMBU & SEAFOOD

INGREDIENTS

150 g/5½ oz cellophane noodles

350 g/12 oz firm-fleshed fish fillets, such as cod, haddock or monkfish, rinsed and cut into bite-sized pieces

1 litre/1¾ pints fish stock or vegetable stock

13-cm/5-inch piece kombu (dried kelp), cut into small pieces and rinsed in cold water

1 tbsp sake

6 tbsp soy sauce

Dippers

4 large peeled carrots, blanched and cut into bite-sized pieces

450 g/1 lb raw prawns, peeled and deveined

300 g/10½ oz sugar snap peas or mangetout, blanched

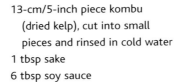

1 Place the noodles in a bowl, cover with cold water and leave to soak for 30 minutes, then drain and cut into 7.5-cm/3-inch lengths. Meanwhile, bring a large saucepan of water to the boil, add the fish pieces and cook briefly for 20 seconds. Drain, rinse under cold water and set aside.

2 Pour the stock into a large saucepan and add the kombu. Bring to the boil, then reduce the heat and simmer for 2 minutes. Pour in the sake. Arrange the reserved fish pieces on serving plates with the other dippers.

3 Pour the stock into a flameproof fondue pot (it should be no more than two-thirds full). Using protective gloves, transfer the fondue pot to a lit tabletop burner. To serve, allow your guests to spear the dippers on to fondue forks or place them on heatproof spoons, dip them into the hot stock until cooked to their taste, then dip them in the soy sauce. When all the dippers have been finished, add the noodles to the stock in the fondue pot and serve as a soup.

CREAMY SAFFRON SCALLOPS

INGREDIENTS

1 kg/2 lb 4 oz live mussels
2 tbsp butter
2 garlic cloves, chopped
4 spring onions, trimmed and chopped
1.2 litres/2 pints dry white wine

125 ml/4 fl oz water
1 bay leaf
250 ml/9 fl oz single cream
½ tsp ground saffron or turmeric
salt and pepper

Dippers
200 g/7 oz raw shelled scallops
selection of blanched vegetables,
    cut into bite-sized pieces

1 Soak the mussels in lightly salted water for 10 minutes, then scrub the shells under cold running water. Pull off any beards. Discard any mussels with broken shells or any that refuse to close when tapped.

2 Melt the butter in a large saucepan over a low heat. Add the garlic and spring onions and cook, stirring, for 3 minutes. Add the wine, water, bay leaf and mussels, bring to the boil and cook over a high heat for 4 minutes, until the mussels have opened. Discard any that remain closed. Strain the mussels, reserving the liquid, and shell them. Discard the bay leaf. Arrange the mussels with the dippers on serving plates.

3 Pour the reserved liquid into a flameproof fondue pot (until two-thirds full). Transfer to the hob and bring to boiling point over a medium heat. Stir in the cream, saffron and salt and pepper to taste. Using protective gloves, transfer the fondue pot to a lit tabletop burner. To serve, allow your guests to spear the dippers on to fondue forks and dip them in the hot fondue for about 3–4 minutes, or until cooked to their taste.

ORIENTAL FIREPOT WITH SEAFOOD DIPPERS

INGREDIENTS

250 g/9 oz fine egg noodles
1.5 litres/2¾ pints fish stock or
    vegetable stock
2 garlic cloves, chopped
2 shallots, chopped
1 tbsp grated fresh root ginger
1 tbsp grated fresh lemon grass
salt and pepper
1 tbsp rice wine or sherry

Dippers
300 g/10½ oz raw prawns, peeled
    and deveined
200 g/7 oz raw shelled scallops
300 g/10½ oz sugar snap peas or
    mangetout, blanched
baby onions, peeled but left whole

1 quantity Oriental Dipping Sauce
    (see page 38), to serve

1 Place the noodles in a heatproof bowl, cover with boiling water and leave to soak for 4 minutes, then drain and set aside. Pour the stock into a large saucepan and add the garlic, shallots, ginger, lemon grass and salt and pepper to taste. Bring to the boil, then reduce the heat and simmer for 15 minutes. Arrange the dippers on serving plates.

2 Stir the rice wine into the stock, then pour into a flameproof fondue pot (it should be no more than two-thirds full). Using protective gloves, transfer the fondue pot to a lit tabletop burner. To serve, allow your guests to spear the dippers on to fondue forks, dip them into the hot stock until cooked to their taste, then dip them in the dipping sauce. When all the dippers have been finished, add the noodles to the stock in the fondue pot and serve as a soup.

PECORINO & CHILLI TUNA SIZZLERS

INGREDIENTS

2 tbsp grated pecorino cheese
2 eggs
5 tbsp plain flour
175 g/6 oz canned tuna, flaked
1 tbsp grated fresh root ginger
1 tbsp grated lemon rind
100 g/3½ oz sweetcorn kernels
½ tsp finely chopped fresh red chilli
1 litre/1¾ pints groundnut oil

Red chilli dipping sauce
125 ml/4 fl oz natural yogurt
4 tbsp mayonnaise
1 fresh red chilli, deseeded and
  finely chopped
1 tbsp lime juice

Dippers
selection of vegetables, cut into
  bite-sized pieces
whole cooked peeled prawns

fresh mixed salad, to serve

1 Put the cheese, eggs and flour into a large bowl and beat together. Add the tuna, ginger, lemon rind, sweetcorn and the ½ teaspoon of chopped red chilli and stir together well. Meanwhile, to make the sauce, put all the ingredients into a non-metallic serving bowl, mix together and set aside. Arrange the dippers on serving plates.

2 Pour the oil into a metal fondue pot (it should be no more than one-third full), then heat on the hob to 190°C/375°F, or until a cube of bread browns in 30 seconds. Using protective gloves, carefully transfer the fondue pot to a lit tabletop burner. To serve, allow your guests to spear the dippers on to fondue forks and cook them with dessertspoonfuls of the tuna mixture in the hot oil for about 3 minutes, or until cooked to their taste. Drain off the excess oil, then serve with the dipping sauce and a mixed salad.

LIME & CHILLI CRAB BALLS

INGREDIENTS

450 g/1 lb frozen crabmeat, thawed
2 tbsp freshly grated lime rind
1 fresh red chilli, deseeded and
   finely chopped
1 tbsp finely chopped spring onion
1 tbsp grated fresh root ginger
1 tbsp grated fresh coconut

2 egg yolks
4 tsp cornflour
4 tbsp thick natural yogurt
2 tbsp sherry
salt and pepper
1 litre/1¾ pints groundnut oil

Dippers
200 g/7 oz firm tofu (drained weight),
   cut into bite-sized pieces
selection of vegetables, cut into
   bite-sized pieces

To serve
1 quantity Oriental Dipping Sauce
   (see page 38)
freshly cooked rice

1 Put the crabmeat, lime rind, chilli, spring onion, ginger, coconut and egg yolk into a bowl and mix together well. Mix the cornflour with the yogurt and sherry in a small saucepan, place over a low heat and stir until thickened. Remove from the heat, mix into the bowl with the crabmeat mixture and season to taste with salt and pepper. Pull off pieces of the mixture and shape into 2.5-cm/1-inch balls. Cover with clingfilm and chill for at least 1 hour. Arrange the other dippers on serving plates.

2 Pour the oil into a metal fondue pot (it should be no more than one-third full), then heat on the hob to 190°C/375°F, or until a cube of bread browns in 30 seconds. Using protective gloves, carefully transfer the fondue pot to a lit tabletop burner. To serve, allow your guests to spear the dippers on to fondue forks (place the crab balls on spoons if not firm enough to spear), then cook in the hot oil for about 2–3 minutes, or until cooked to their taste. Drain off the excess oil, then serve with the dipping sauce and rice.

dessert fondues

There is no better way to round off a meal than with a luxuriously indulgent sweet fondue. Chocolate lovers will adore the Brandy Chocolate with Fruit Dippers (see page 88) and the Mocha with Amaretti (see page 94), and Nutty Butterscotch with Popcorn (see page 84) will prove irresistible to children and adults alike. For those of you who would like to add an extra sizzle to your meal's finale, the Chocolate Wontons with Maple Sauce (see page 90) will capture everyone's imagination and have the whole household clamouring for more.

NUTTY BUTTERSCOTCH WITH POPCORN

INGREDIENTS

350 g/12 oz brown sugar
125 ml/4 fl oz water
1 tbsp rum
6 tbsp unsalted butter
125 ml/4 fl oz double cream,
   gently warmed
85 g/3 oz peanuts, chopped

Dippers
popcorn
firm ripe bananas, cut into
   bite-sized pieces
sliced apples

1 Arrange the dippers decoratively on a serving platter or individual serving plates and set aside.

2 Put the sugar and water into a heavy-based saucepan, place over a medium heat and stir until the sugar has dissolved. Bring to the boil, then leave to bubble for 6–7 minutes. Stir in the rum and cook for another minute.

3 Using protective gloves, remove from the heat and carefully stir in the butter until melted. Gradually stir in the cream until the mixture is smooth. Finally, stir in the nuts.

4 Carefully pour the mixture into a warmed fondue pot, then transfer to a lit tabletop burner. To serve, allow your guests to spear the dippers on to fondue forks and dip them into the fondue.

CREAMY RUM WITH BANANA

INGREDIENTS

125 g/4½ oz caster sugar
4 tbsp water
350 ml/12 fl oz double cream,
    gently warmed
3 tbsp rum

Dippers

plain sponge cake, cut into
    bite-sized pieces
firm ripe bananas, cut into
    bite-sized pieces
sliced apples

1 Arrange the dippers decoratively on a serving platter or individual serving plates and set aside.

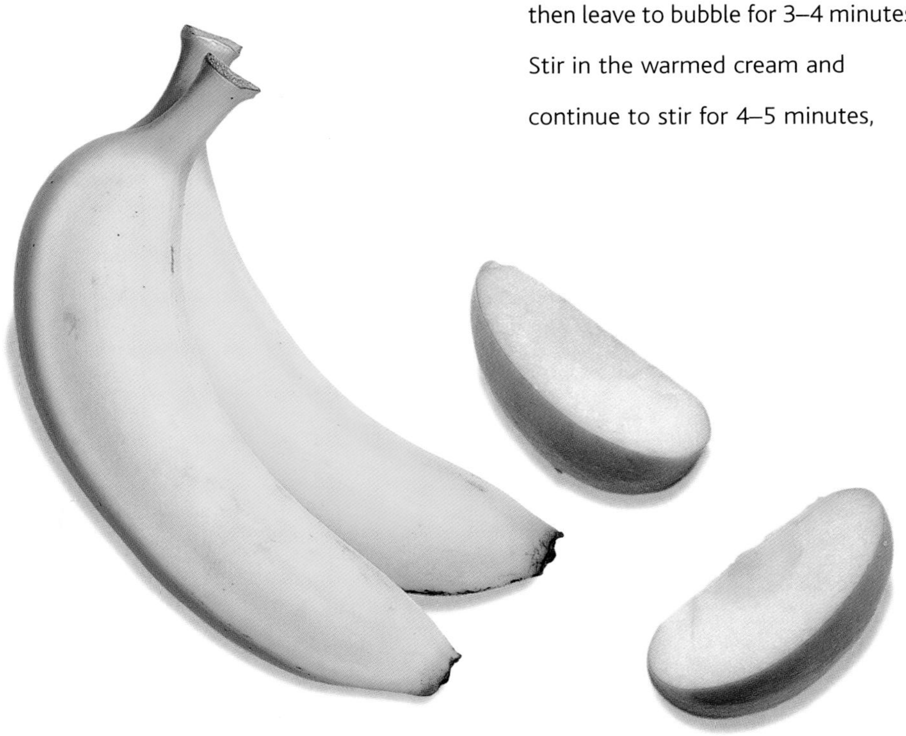

2 Put the sugar and water into a heavy-based saucepan, place over a low heat and stir until the sugar has dissolved. Bring to the boil, then leave to bubble for 3–4 minutes. Stir in the warmed cream and continue to stir for 4–5 minutes, until smooth and well combined. Stir in the rum and cook for another minute. Remove from the heat and carefully pour the mixture into a warmed fondue pot.

3 Using protective gloves, transfer the fondue pot to a lit tabletop burner. To serve, allow your guests to spear the dippers on to fondue forks and dip them into the fondue.

BRANDY CHOCOLATE WITH FRUIT DIPPERS

INGREDIENTS

250 g/9 oz plain chocolate
   (must contain at least
   50 per cent cocoa solids)
100 ml/3½ fl oz double cream
2 tbsp brandy

Dippers
plain sponge cake, cut into
   bite-sized pieces
small pink and white marshmallows
small firm whole fresh fruits, such as
   blackcurrants, blueberries, cherries
   and strawberries
whole no-soak dried apricots
crystallized citrus peel, cut
   decoratively into strips or
   bite-sized pieces

1 Arrange the dippers decoratively on a serving platter or individual serving plates and set aside.

2 Break or chop the chocolate into small pieces and place in the top of a double boiler or in a heatproof bowl set over a saucepan of simmering water. Pour in the cream and stir until melted and smooth. Stir in the brandy, then carefully pour the mixture into a warmed fondue pot.

3 Using protective gloves, transfer the fondue pot to a lit tabletop burner. To serve, allow your guests to spear the dippers on to fondue forks and dip into the fondue.

CHOCOLATE WONTONS WITH MAPLE SAUCE

INGREDIENTS

16 wonton wrappers
350 g/12 oz plain chocolate, chopped
1 tbsp cornflour
3 tbsp cold water
1 litre/1¾ pints groundnut oil

Maple sauce
175 ml/6 fl oz maple syrup
4 tbsp butter
½ tsp ground mixed spice

vanilla ice cream, to serve

1 Spread out the wonton wrappers on a clean work surface, then spoon a little chopped chocolate into the centre of each wrapper. In a small bowl, mix together the cornflour and water until smooth. Brush the edges of the wrappers with the cornflour mixture, then wrap in any preferred shape, such as triangles, squares or bundles, and seal the edges. Arrange the wontons on a serving platter.

2 To make the maple sauce, put all the ingredients into a saucepan and stir over a medium heat. Bring to the boil, then reduce the heat and simmer for 3 minutes.

3 Meanwhile, pour the oil into a metal fondue pot (it should be no more than one-third full), then heat on the hob to 190°C/375°F, or until a cube of bread browns in 30 seconds. Using protective gloves, carefully transfer the fondue pot to a lit tabletop burner.

4 To serve, allow your guests to place the wontons on metal spoons (or spear on to fondue forks) and dip them into the hot oil until cooked to their taste (they will need about 2–3 minutes). Drain off the excess oil, then serve with vanilla ice cream and the sauce.

VANILLA TOFFEE

INGREDIENTS

125 g/4½ oz butter
400 g/14 oz brown sugar
225 ml/8 fl oz golden syrup
2 tbsp maple syrup
2 tbsp water
400 ml/14 fl oz canned condensed milk
1 tsp vanilla extract
½ tsp ground cinnamon
1 tbsp rum

Dippers
sweet biscuits
firm ripe bananas, cut into
    bite-sized pieces
sliced apples
bite-sized pieces of chocolate
miniature fairy cakes
shelled nuts, such as pecan or Brazil
    nuts, and walnut halves

1 Arrange the dippers decoratively on a serving platter or individual serving plates and set aside.

2 Put the butter into a heatproof bowl set over a saucepan of simmering water and melt gently. Add the sugar, golden syrup, maple syrup, water, condensed milk, vanilla extract and cinnamon. Stir until thickened and smooth, then stir in the rum and cook for another minute. Remove from the heat and carefully pour the mixture into a warmed fondue pot.

3 Using protective gloves, transfer the fondue pot to a lit tabletop burner. To serve, allow your guests to spear the dippers on to fondue forks and dip them into the fondue.

MOCHA WITH AMARETTI

INGREDIENTS

250 g/9 oz plain chocolate
   (must contain at least
   50 per cent cocoa solids)
100 ml/3½ fl oz double cream
1 tbsp instant coffee powder
3 tbsp coffee-flavoured liqueur,
   such as Kahlúa

Dippers
sweet biscuits, such as amaretti
plain or coffee-flavoured marbled
   cake or sponge cake, cut into
   bite-sized pieces
whole seedless grapes
sliced firm peaches or nectarines

1 Arrange the dippers decoratively on a serving platter or individual serving plates and set aside.

2 Break or chop the chocolate into small pieces and place in the top of a double boiler or in a heatproof bowl set over a saucepan of simmering water. Add the cream and coffee powder and stir until melted and smooth. Stir in the liqueur, then carefully pour the mixture into a warmed fondue pot.

3 Using protective gloves, transfer the fondue pot to a lit tabletop burner. To serve, allow your guests to spear the dippers on to fondue forks and dip them into the hot fondue.

index